PHILLIP H

# Adventures
## With the Holy Spirit

*This book is dedicated to all those who, "bear one another's burdens, and so fulfill the law of Christ."* (GALATIANS 6:2, KJV)

PHILLIP HALVERSON
MARCH 15, 1917 — JUNE 2, 1985

# Introduction

I believe the essence of the New Testament can be summed up in this statement: "Take care of *others* and God will take care of *you*."

Intercessory prayer is for *others*.

I have had numerous astonishing experiences in intercessory prayer. Through this book I would like to share them with you, that you may know how alive and active the Holy Spirit is, bringing forth God's purposes in the earth today.

# Contents

PHILLIP HALVERSON

# Adventures
## With the Holy Spirit

# 1
# A Sense of Destiny

A divine discontent began to possess me and Fern. A great yearning filled us, a longing to be absolutely controlled by the Holy Spirit.

Both of us had worked in our local Assembly of God church since our youth, but we were in a static place in our Christian experience. The plateau we lived on had no new horizons. It seemed we were simply maintaining the "status-quo," and all of our friends appeared to be in a similar condition.

Our lives began to change in 1962, when our pastor invited us to join him in opening a downtown mission, completely separate from our church. He resigned his pastorate and rented what had formerly been a large burlesque theater in downtown Minneapolis. This outreach soon was thriving. Every night of the week three balconies were filled to overflowing, as throngs of seekers found hope and peace in Jesus. Fern and I worked together at the altar and in the prayer room. We also conducted follow-up teaching for the new converts in seminars explaining, "What's Happened to Me?"

Imagine the needs of these dear converts, attempting to start a new life. For some, simple things like food and clothing meant survival. Our hearts were touched with the challenge of ministering to these new brothers and sisters.

How well I remember the day Fern and I were discussing our desire to help others, and measuring it against our budget. There simply was not enough money to meet the needs of both.

We determined that day to take God at His Word. In Luke 6:38, He said;

*Give, and it shall be given unto you; good measure,*
*pressed down, and shaken together, and running*
*over, shall men give into your bosom. For with the*
*same measure that ye mete withal it shall be mea-*
*sured to you again.* (KJV)

And again in Malachi 3:10, He says;

*Bring ye all the tithes into the storehouse...and prove*
*me now herewith, saith the Lord of hosts, if I will*
*not open you the windows of heaven, and pour you*
*out a blessing, that there shall not be room enough*
*to receive it.* (KJV)

We had always tithed, but now we were eager to expand the scope of our lives.

Suddenly, a joyous abandonment filled us! Why not immediately begin to tithe as if we *already* had the increase we wanted in our income? We had never heard of this being done, but were certain that God would honor our step of faith. We felt like pioneers launching forth into a new dimension.

I can guess what you might be thinking; *Someone died and left us a fortune?...We discovered oil in our backyard?...We uncovered a cache of diamonds in our attic?"*

No!

The *unique gifts of the Holy Spirit* began to operate. From that day forward, events were set in motion that changed the course of our lives.

The first thing that occurred was a very close and intimate fellowship with the Father. Our financial commitment led us to lean heavily on His breast. We felt the heaving of His love, and that breath of the Spirit of God became preciously close.

It was a time of awe—to be in the very presence of God! We were filled with the certain knowledge that He is

9

God of every situation. A sense of destiny overwhelmed us, and became a consuming desire to walk in a greater dimension of His Holy Spirit.

Intercessory prayer began to develop and operate within us, together with the word of wisdom and the word of knowledge. (The word of knowledge pertains to former and present persons, circumstances or events; the word of wisdom has to do with the future.)

This was the beginning of miraculous happenings! God was fulfilling His promise to us from Jeremiah 29:13-14;

> *Then you will seek Me, inquire for and require Me [as a vital necessity] and find Me; when you search for Me with all your heart, I will be found by you, says the Lord.*

# 2
# Divine Arrangements

All our crops burned out when I was eighteen years old, and there were ten hungry mouths to feed in our family. This was during the Great Depression and the whole community was suffering. What was there to do?

My cousin Enoch had been to North Dakota to work in the harvest fields, and he knew a farmer who needed four men. Enoch had room for a fifth passenger, but no promise of work. I wanted to be on my own and was convinced that I should be that passenger. So after borrowing five dollars from my uncle and packing a suitcase, I went on a real adventure.

Before dawn, some six hundred miles later, Enoch dropped me off in a tiny town in North Dakota. Then he and the others departed to report for their jobs.

It was still dark, and I sat down on the steps of a small store in that group of six antique buildings feeling very alone. I had spent most of my money and had no way to get back home. So I did the only thing I knew to do—I prayed. Although I had not yet experienced the baptism of the Holy Spirit, I did know the Lord and gratefully rested in His conscious presence. I asked Him to open up a job for me. I didn't have long to wait!

Just as daylight was approaching, two men in an old car pulled up right in front of me. They knew of a farmer down the road who needed help. I gave them my last few cents to drive me out to this farm. On the way, I noticed that a freight train ran right by the farm. The tops of the boxcars were covered with bums who had no jobs and no other way of transportation.

Walking into the farmyard, I inquired if they could use some help. "Yes!" came the reply, "We are going to need a large crew, as our crops are excellent." I put my small suitcase down in the corner of a machinery shed and went to work right then.

At noon I was invited into the farmhouse for dinner, though I noted that other farmhands were served in the bunkhouse area. Can you imagine my joy when the farmer gave thanks to the Lord for the food—and for sending me?

He also announced that they would have a church meeting in the house that evening and that anyone who wanted to come was invited. I was thrilled to see how the hand of God had directed me to the home of real Christians. Of the crew of twenty men, only one other young man, Richard Palmer, attended the meeting with me that evening.

After some songs and a sermon, there was a time of earnest prayer. I watched with amazement as the other young man, Richard, was filled with the Holy Spirit. (Dick is now a veteran Assembly of God missionary to Peru.)

This was my first evening at this farm, so I asked where I should sleep. The farmer said, "I have two sons in one double bed upstairs and Dick is in another double bed. Why don't you share with Dick instead of sleeping in the bunkhouse?"

All my pre-dawn apprehensions had vanished! By nightfall I had a job, good food, clean quarters and Christian fellowship—more than I would have ever dreamed.

After about a week, the farmer told me he would like to find more workers like me. Remembering the tops of those boxcars filled with men needing work, I wrote home. My father came to work for about two months, along with several men of our church. Money was provided for the harsh winters of 1935 and 1936, which were among the coldest ever recorded.

In 1937, I joined the choir at my church, and soon noticed a lovely girl playing the piano. Her name was Fern Pihl, and she had been the church pianist since she was fourteen years of age. After a courtship of three years, we were married. Eight months later I was drafted into the

U.S. Army for a year. Nine months after that, Pearl Harbor was bombed, and I served until the war was over. After the war, we established our home in Minneapolis where we were active in our church serving in many capacities. Like Abraham's servant, I could say;

*...I being in the way [of obedience and faith], the Lord led me...* (Genesis 24:27)

# 3
# Utterances

It wasn't until I was married and had a child that I was baptized with the Holy Spirit and first spoke in that heavenly language (tongues). I began to pray in tongues, not only at my home, but also in church and at home prayer meetings.

I Corinthians 14:14, accurately describes my experience at that time;

> *For if I pray in an unknown tongue, my spirit*
> *prayeth, but my understanding is unfruitful.* (KJV)

I often felt the Holy Spirit moving me to prayer, and I gave myself to that urge. It didn't matter where I was—in the performance of my job, driving my car, reading my Bible, even while listening to someone speak in meetings—I found myself breathing prayers in tongues to God.

I knew this prayer was on behalf of others, because I had been taught about the work of the Holy Spirit, and I *felt the need of others* when I prayed. Of course, in my natural mind I had no idea what to pray for—only to pray. When others asked me to pray, I would do so, and often utterances in tongues would come forth.

I also prayed with my understanding, making my requests known to God with words I could understand. Then that helper, the Holy Spirit, came to assist me in my prayer with supernatural utterances in tongues. It was a real release. Romans 8:26 tells us;

> *...the Spirit Himself goes to meet our supplication,*
> *and pleads in our behalf with unspeakable yearn-*
> *ings and groanings too deep for utterance.*

Yes, as I prayed in the Spirit, groanings did come forth but sometimes, to my amazement, *English words* came forth as well! I was puzzled. Why did *English words* come forth as I prayed in *tongues?*

I inquired of my pastor. He had not heard of a similar experience, but assured me that the Holy Spirit was bringing forth these English words. This did give me a measure of comfort, but my natural mind was still puzzled.

John 16:13-14, began to take on new meaning to me;

> *But when He, the Spirit of Truth (the truth-giving Spirit) comes, He will guide you into all the truth... He will tell whatever He hears [from the Father, He will give the message that has been given to Him] and He will announce and declare to you the things that are to come--that will happen in the future.*

The King James version puts it this way;

> *Howbeit when he, the Spirit of truth is come, he will guide you into all truth: for he shall not speak of himself; but whatsoever he shall hear, that shall He speak: and he will shew you things to come. He shall glorify me: for he shall receive of mine, and shall shew it unto you.*

The Spirit of truth was dwelling richly in me, guiding even the *words I uttered* in prayer. As I followed His leading, my prayer life continued to expand in astonishing ways.

# 4
# The Hearse
# Without a Corpse

I was putting the finishing touches of polish on my car while awaiting the arrival of Brad and Jean, out-of-state friends. They had phoned that morning to say they would only have time for a quick cup of coffee.

The coffee was perking and the light lunch was ready for the table when they arrived. Brad and I talked briefly in the garage while Jean and Fern visited in the kitchen.

Jean shared with Fern her concern for a friend, Mrs. Edwards, the wife of their local mortician. Mr. Edwards had found his wife unconscious on the bathroom floor and rushed her to the small local hospital. They could do nothing for her, so she was transferred to a larger hospital about fifty miles away, and then transferred again to the Mayo Clinic in Rochester, Minnesota. Doctors at Mayo determined that she had suffered an inoperable brain aneurysm, and informed her husband that her condition was hopeless. Mr. Edwards was told that the hospital would call when it was time for him to pick up her body.

A very sad Mr. Edwards had shared this with Jean and Brad. As they finished setting the table, Jean told Fern, "Be sure to pray for them."

Their schedule was tight, so when Brad and I came inside we finished a quick lunch, prayed together, and bade them Godspeed on their return trip.

Later that night, Fern was awakened to hear me uttering a mighty prayer in the Holy Spirit in tongues. The tongues were forceful; *then came English words*: "Intervene for Mrs. Edwards! Intervene for the aneurysm!" Over and over again the Holy Spirit spoke these words.

When the prayer had subsided, Fern exclaimed, "That must be the Mrs. Edwards that Jean was talking about today!"

"What Mrs. Edwards?" I asked. "Who is Mrs. Edwards? What about her?" (Fern hadn't mentioned her conversation with Jean, thinking Brad had probably discussed it with me.)

"Didn't Brad tell you about their mortician's wife?"

"No, what about her? Tell me!"

Fern proceeded to relate to me the brief history Jean had given her. Then we continued to pray for this Mrs. Edwards with our natural understanding, commanding the aneurysm to be dissolved in Jesus' name. We held Mrs. Edwards up to the Father with thanks and praise for her deliverance, claiming perfect wholeness for her body, with no after-effects from this episode. After praying fervently in this fashion for perhaps half an hour, we slept soundly and awakened the next morning, refreshed.

Not that day, but the following day, I got a call from an excited Brad.

"Phil, I have to tell you what has happened to our friend, Mrs. Edwards!" he exclaimed.

"Oh, tell us! We want to hear," I replied.

"Well," continued Brad, "Yesterday the Mayo Clinic called Mr. Edwards and told him to come and pick up his wife. He drove the hearse to Rochester with a heavy heart, expecting to pick up her dead body. But as he entered the lobby, he thought he saw a vision to his left. *Was that his wife sitting there, all dressed?* Walking toward her, he was ecstatic to find that it was indeed his wife! She knew nothing about her former condition, except what the doctors had told her when she was discharged!"

I then told Brad about the astonishing prayer I experienced the night after he and Jean had left our house. The Holy Spirit had intervened in a mighty way! We were both almost breathless!

Fern and I were filled with amazement, and wanted to verify this tremendous miracle. The following weekend we drove to Brad and Jean's community in another state and

17

visited firsthand with Mr. and Mrs. Edwards. We found a very grateful (and still incredulous) husband and his happy, vibrant, very-much-alive wife.

As the Lord says in Jeremiah 1:12;

> *...I am alert and active, watching over My word to perform it.*

# 5
# Mr. Crawford

We were driving along the freeway, returning from another state, and were about fifteen miles from home. The tape player in our car had been feeding us God's Word, and we were rejoicing in the goodness of the Lord.

I kept hearing the voice of the Spirit telling me that I would be in the hospital as a patient with intravenous feeding. Along with that, the word "Crawford" occurred frequently in prayer.

When I shared this with Fern, she rejected that thought. "Oh no!" she said, "We believe in divine healing, and you are not going to be in any hospital!"

That quiet inner voice continued, however, as well as intercession of the Holy Spirit. The voice was inaudible, but very certain.

Less than a week later, I awoke one morning with intense pain. Going into the living room, I proceeded to read my Bible and talk with the Lord, but soon was doubled up with pain. Fern discovered me rolling and groaning on the floor.

We did not have a family doctor, so Fern called her brother for advice, and soon I found myself being admitted to a hospital. The unremitting pain was so intense that I cannot describe it.

No sooner had a nurse attached an intravenous feeding tube to my arm than the pain stopped abruptly, and was replaced by the most fantastic feeling of peace I have ever known. It was as though I was floating on air.

Fern and I reminded one another of the car ride and the word of knowledge that had come forth concerning this. We sensed that I must be in that hospital for some specific purpose, and knew this was a time to look for the unexpected.

Sharing my room was a man who had been there for weeks. His extremely high blood pressure was not responding to treatment and he was getting progressively worse. He informed me that his wife was in another hospital for treatment of a back disorder.

"My name," he said, "is Crawford."

*Crawford!* That was the word that had occurred frequently in prayer! I knew that I was in the right place at the right time.

Meanwhile I felt fine, though I was tested for just about everything. I was simply waiting for the tests to be completed so I could go home, but friends came to visit and pray with me anyway, including my pastor. As he was about to pray for me, Mr. Crawford called across the room, "Don't pray for him; *I'm* the one who needs prayer!"

It is my joy to tell you that Mr. Crawford found Jesus as his Savior that very hour. By the end of that week, he had improved so much that his doctors said he could go home. No sooner had his doctors left the room, than my doctor came in to say that I could go home too. (They could find nothing wrong with me; all my tests were perfect!)

As it turned out, Mr. Crawford's wife was discharged that morning also. He insisted that they drive me home, instead of Fern coming to pick me up. They lived in our general area, so I accepted.

Later, over a cup of fresh coffee, Fern had the privilege and joy of sharing God's love with Mrs. Crawford who eagerly accepted Christ as her Savior too!

The Lord had truly directed our paths according to Proverbs 3:5-6;

> *Lean on, trust, and be confident in the Lord with all your heart and mind, and do not rely on your own insight or understanding. In all your ways know, recognize, and acknowledge Him, and He will direct and make straight and plain your paths.*

# 6
# The Great Alaskan Earthquake

We were part of a prayer group that met regularly to pray for individual requests, and also to rejoice over the answers we received. What times of refreshing! These people loved to pray, and would intercede with groanings and travail until the peace of God replaced a particular burden. We shared each others' concerns in united prayer—some sitting, some standing, some lying on the floor.

Usually we met on a Friday night at one anothers' homes. All of us arrived eager to share together. One particular evening in 1964, we had been in earnest prayer for several hours when I found myself abandoned to prayer and groaning in the Holy Spirit. Suddenly, English words came forth; "At about dusk...at about dusk...at about dusk...." The Holy Spirit went on to describe a terrible shaking and devastating destruction, naming many cities in Alaska. The fifteen or twenty of us assembled that night will never forget it.

Early the next morning, I received many excited telephone calls.

"Have you seen the morning paper?" a friend asked.

"I don't take the paper," I replied.

The great Alaskan earthquake had occurred the night before. The newspaper articles began with the very words, "At about dusk...."

The word of knowledge had been in operation at that prayer meeting. Some might ask, "What good did it do? It didn't prevent the earthquake."

God had a purpose in revealing it to me at that meeting, and it did have significance for a man named

21

George. A rather new Christian, George was present with his wife that night. He had been mightily filled with the Holy Spirit and we were thrilled to see the gifts of the Spirit coming into operation in his life.

George had been considering associating himself with some men in a business and had even come to my home with some of them for prayer. I had prayed with George several times and warned him that the Holy Spirit strongly impressed me that he was not to go into this business. I agonized so much for George in prayer that I would call him on the phone and beg him not to get involved in this proposed business.

One day I could not get my work done because of the tremendous burden of travail in prayer for George. My advice and tears brought no action.

But George was at the prayer meeting on that Friday night. As far as I can ascertain, God had established my credibility with a true word of knowledge that night (as well as other times that George was aware of). Sadly, he chose to go into this endeavor anyway only to find the Holy Spirit's warnings to be true. The business was a failure, spiritually draining, not God's will for him and, ultimately, a spiritual setback.

This is a rare instance. I do not pray with people to ascertain God's will for them. Only if God burdens me in a definite area do I contact the people involved and inform them of the concern of the Holy Spirit.

*Therefore be always alert and on your guard, being mindful that for three years I never stopped night or day seriously to admonish and advise and exhort you one by one with tears.* (Acts 20:31)

# 7
# Donald Oman

Many times I pray off and on through the night hours. Fern usually awakens as I drift in and out of prayer.

On this particular night, I heard myself praying for a "Donald Oman." I prayed for the intervention of the Holy Spirit several times in a very authoritative voice. Then in a decisive, loud command, I spoke these words;

"DONALD OMAN! IN THE NAME OF JESUS CHRIST, STAND UP! LIVE! IN THE NAME OF JESUS, LIVE! LIVE TO FINISH THE WORK I HAVE FOR YOU TO DO!"

We were both fully awake now. A holy awe filled the room as we realized the Holy Spirit was active on behalf of someone very ill whom we did not know.

A few months passed, and we were visiting a church we had formerly attended. We were astonished to see the name, "Donald Oman," on a prayer list that was distributed prior to the meeting.

After the meeting, we inquired for the person who had compiled that weekly prayer list. "About this Donald Oman," we asked, "Who is he?"

"Oh!" she said, "His mother-in-law is in the meeting this morning." We found her and told her of the outstanding prayer in the Holy Spirit we had experienced. And this is what she told us.

Donald Oman was her son-in-law, a missionary to Lebanon in charge of an orphanage. He had been ill for some time struggling between life and death and had finally succumbed. Efforts to revive him were fruitless.

Because of the climate in that country, plans were made for his immediate cremation. As they were preparing, his wife cried out, "Oh, God! Spare Don! Please, God, spare my husband!"

At that precise moment, visible signs of life began to be manifest in his body and shortly he revived, weak but alive.

We ascertained the time of this miracle to be the exact hour of the intercession of the Holy Spirit in our bedroom, even to the night and time-zone difference!

Donald Oman came back to this country to regain his health. He did live many years and finished the work the Lord had ordained for him. We recently had the privilege of preaching in the church he founded in America.

> *...the Holy Spirit comes to our aid and bears us up in our weakness; for we do not know what prayer to offer nor how to offer it worthily as we ought, but the Spirit Himself goes to meet our supplication and pleads in our behalf with unspeakable yearnings and groanings too deep for utterance. And He Who searches the hearts of men knows what is in the mind of the (Holy) Spirit --what His intent is-- because the Spirit intercedes and pleads [before God] in behalf of the saints according to and in harmony with God's will.* (Romans 8:26-27)

# 8
# For Sale
# by Owner

A business we developed had grown necessitating opening another office in an adjoining city. After about six months there, the office building we occupied was sold, and we discovered we would have to vacate in two months.

We were in a great area in terms of both business and transportation, and the task of finding comparable space at affordable rent was a challenge.

As usual, my prayer life included the heavenly language in tongues and in songs, as well as prayers in English. I interceded for many situations and persons, but lately had been aware of the name "Miller" coming forth. More and more frequently I heard the name "Miller" in prayer with an urgency in the Holy Spirit. Of course, I did not even think to connect it with our need for office space.

The search began. Fern checked out several places that were available, but none were in the location we desired, nor were they suitable for our business.

I had casually noticed a building directly across the street from our office, but it was "For Sale by Owner." When I suggested to Fern that she should check it out, she reminded me, "We surely don't want to buy a building." Still, I walked across the street to investigate further.

It had several office spaces we could possibly rent out in addition to plenty of space for ourselves and a large basement. I persuaded Fern to look it over.

The man who showed it to us was the nephew of the owner. He explained that his uncle was ill, and did not want to rent it out. The building was vacant, and he wanted to dispose of it.

We had no intention of purchasing a building, but

finally thought to ask what the price of the building might be. When he told us the price, we couldn't believe we had uncovered such a bargain! And the Holy Spirit was nudging us about the urgency of the situation.

I was so impressed to get going with the purchase that I had our attorney draw up the papers that afternoon and give them to the owner's nephew.

That was Friday.

On Monday morning we met with the owner's nephew. All the papers were signed and in order, and as he handed them to us, he told us his uncle had passed away that morning. Glancing at the papers, I was startled to
realize that his uncle's name was *Miller!* That was the first time we heard his name other than by the Holy Spirit in prayer.

We owned that building for many years. When we felt a change coming, the Lord sent a buyer not only for that building but also for our business. (That is a story of countless miracles all its own!)

> *And my God will liberally supply (fill to the full)*
> *your every need according to His riches in glory in*
> *Christ Jesus.* (Philippians 4:19)

# 9
# Ivar

I was raking our yard and had been praying in the Holy Spirit. The name "Ivar" was coming forth frequently as I prayed. Suddenly I remembered that a friend of Fern's father named Ivar was in a coma at the local Veterans' Hospital. I put my yard rake aside and headed to the back door to tell Fern I felt we should go to see Ivar.

At the same moment, Fern emerged from the kitchen door. "Phil, could we go out to the hospital today and pray for Ivar? I am so impressed to visit him today. You know he is unsaved as far as we know."

The nurse on duty at his floor told us he had been comatose for two weeks, had no visitors and gave no response. She left to perform her other duties.

We were just outside Ivar's door so we tiptoed in. He was alone, sleeping in a six-bed room. He looked ashen— dead.

Leaning over his bed, Fern gently touched Ivar on the shoulder. "Ivar, Ivar, we have come to talk to you and pray with you." Ivar's eyes opened suddenly and, as Fern leaned over him, their eyes met. Softly, Fern said, "Ivar, we have come to tell you that God loves you and gave Jesus to be your Savior. Do you know who I am?"

We were startled to hear a reply! "Yes, you are Rudy's daughter, Fern."

This man had been in a coma for two weeks! Now he was awake and actually speaking to us! While his response was slow, his words were accurate. We were astounded to realize that we were witnessing a miracle.

I gently took Ivar's hand as I prayed. "Father, reveal Yourself to Ivar now as Jesus' blood cleanses him from every sin, and he becomes a child of God."

We were about to leave, but hadn't taken more than a few steps toward the door when we heard his voice. We turned to see him raised up on one elbow. Returning to his bed we heard him say slowly, "Th... thanks a lot, th... thanks a lot, folks." We were awed.

Those were his last words, as he went to be with his Savior that very night. I am touched afresh when I tell you this event.

*[Besides these evidences] it was also established and plainly endorsed by God, Who showed His approval of it by signs and wonders and various miraculous manifestations of [His] power and by imparting the gifts of the Holy Spirit [to the believers] according to His own will.* (Hebrews 2:4)

# 10
# "Censored!"

"Censored! Censored! Censored!" I heard these words over and over again as I prayed. I would pray in tongues often with travail, and then these English words would come forth.

One day a letter arrived. A word was stamped across the face of it in big black letters:

"CENSORED."

Spiritual alert sounded.

"Dear Mr. and Mrs. Halverson," it began, "Jack M., an inmate of this prison, has requested contact with you. If you do not wish to have contact, do not respond to this letter. If you do wish to correspond, please acknowledge on the enclosed card and send to...."

We responded that we were honored to be counted as a friend of this young inmate, and very shortly received a long letter from Jack.

He had been in my Sunday school class many years before. His whole family had been saved and brought many relatives and friends who also found Jesus as their personal Savior. But the family moved to New York to begin a new business and did not find the Christian fellowship they desperately needed. We had lost contact with them for many years.

Jack's brilliant mind got him into trouble and eventually his career in crime landed him behind bars. Seeking to end his life, he slashed his wrists, but survived to live with guilt and despair.

One day in solitary confinement, agony overwhelmed him and he cried out in desperation, "Oh God! Send someone to me! Help me! God, Oh God, help me!"

Suddenly the image of our faces appeared before him. He knew unmistakably that God would send us to him, and his request led the prison officials to contact us.

We wrote him how honored we were to be counted as his friends. We were touched with his story, and wanted him to know that we would do everything we could to be a strength to him and to stand by him and his family. We assured him of our prayers and of the Holy Spirit's intercession for him. He was encouraged though still desperately depressed. We wanted to see him.

Jack certainly did have problems. Not only was he incarcerated, but his wife Joyce was pressing for a divorce. His letters to her were returned unopened causing him great torment. His furniture was repossessed, his new car was hauled off for non-payment, and there was no money for the mortgage payments either.

Now there is a certain fascination in knowing that the Holy Spirit has breathed on a situation. You don't know how in the wide world things are going to turn out right, but you do know that you have a part to play, and that God will deliver. We were confidently expectant and wanted to obey the Lord though it certainly did not seem like a fortuitous adventure.

The letters poured back and forth between us. Every day Fern would sit down to the typewriter with nothing fresh to say, and every day God would give her the scriptures and encouraging words that Jack needed to hear. He was absolutely sick about losing his wife and young son.

The evening is memorable that Fern and I stopped to meet Joyce and their four-year-old son, Greg. Joyce was bitter against her husband, and didn't want us to talk to her about him. We asked her how we could help, and whether she had a Bible. When we told her that her husband had accepted Jesus as his Savior as a boy, she left the room. We were surprised to see her return with a Bible.

We read scriptures and presented Christ as the only

answer, but it seemed that Joyce responded indifferently. When asked if she would accept Jesus in her situation, she said she couldn't pray, but then repeated a prayer after Fern. Then in another surprising turn, she called her son over and said, "Greggy, you pray like Mommy did."

We urged her to begin reading the book of John and added that we wanted to keep track of her by stopping in, phoning, and having her and Greg in our home for dinner and some overnight weekends.

Fern in particular had a special grace to reach out to Joyce persistently with the love of Jesus. At times it seemed that Joyce had repeated that initial prayer only to be polite. The animosity she voiced toward her husband gave the impression that the Word of God had not been sown in good ground. But Fern was determined to nourish that ground so it could bear fruit knowing this was God's will.

Stopping by her home one afternoon with a couple of sweet rolls for coffee, Fern chatted with Joyce, read scripture and asked if she would please reconsider her attitude toward her husband. His letters were always returned to him unopened, and he so wanted to communicate with her. But walls of offense had long before been built and reinforced in Joyce's heart.

When asked how she was coming along with her Bible reading, Joyce replied, "I just don't get anything out of it."

Fern gently reminded Joyce that Jesus said, "If you *continue* in My Word, then you are My disciples indeed; and you shall know the truth, and the truth shall make you free." (John 8:31-32, KJV)

Then Fern explained to Joyce that the first way to obey the Lord is to show love. "I wonder, Joyce, how you can show God you really want to obey Him and to partake of His freedom?"

It was very quiet. Joyce had nothing to say.

"I know," Fern continued prayerfully, "You have

it tough right now, but think of your husband in prison. He has it a lot tougher. Just to show a glimmer of concern (Fern didn't dare use the word *love*) to another human being who is worse off than you are, why not, just out of pity, send him a note?"

There was absolutely no response. Fern headed for home.

While Fern was preparing the evening meal for guests, the phone rang. "Hello. This is Joyce." (It was the first phone call we had ever received from her!) "Well, I... well, I just... uh... I just came from the... uh... corner drugstore ...and ...uh ...I mailed a short... uh... note to... Jack."

That's when we knew Joyce had the spark of God living within her! She had deliberately determined to obey the glimmer of light she saw at the far end of the tunnel.
It was all she could do at that point, but thank God she did it!

Fern was more determined than ever to fan that spark. In her own way, Joyce had made a baby step toward God, and now God would take a giant step to aid her!

All this time, I continued to pray much in the Spirit about, "Censored!"

One night we took Joyce and Greg to an ice show. On another occasion, we were dropping them off after a special concert at our church. Knowing that their finances were desperate, I handed Joyce some money.

The next day Fern was nearby and stopped in to see her. Joyce had been to a hairdresser and had the fanciest hairdo Fern had ever seen–complete with several hair-pieces. Fern's first thought was, "Joyce, you and I are going to have a little talk about the value of money!" But she found that it wouldn't come out that way. Instead, Fern found herself saying, "My, Joyce, you look just beautiful! Your hair is gorgeous!"

On the way home, Fern was so thankful that she hadn't let the flesh come out to scold Joyce. And that was the beginning of a real change in her relationship, not only with us, but with her husband.

During the next few months, communication opened up between Jack and Joyce. He wrote us volumes. His letters to us were full of praise and expectancy about his future, which he had now committed totally to the Lord. He announced that he was filled with the Holy Spirit and spoke in that heavenly language. "I am now a free man, even in prison!" he exclaimed.

Jack's enrollment in Bible correspondence courses resulted in a wall full of graduation certificates, with an A+ in every course. (I know, because I later had them framed for his new home.) His appearance also changed dramatically. He formerly had bloody, bitten nails, bloodshot eyes and nervous, jerky motions. Now he was a self-confident, eager-to-learn, eager-to-please, well-groomed young man anyone would be proud to know.

We didn't see Jack often as he was allowed only two visits per month, and we wanted them to be with his family. But we were at the prison often anyway as the chaplain had invited us to conduct some early Sunday services and to substitute occasionally when he was out of town.

The pardon board had reviewed Jack's record and said they would not allow a parole. In addition, his family's lawyers had tried and couldn't get anyone to budge for a parole. We had even met before the pardon board with our pastor, but Jack's long sentence appeared to have no chance of being shortened for any reason.

In the meantime, Joyce was still seeing her divorce lawyer, and Jack's relatives were upset over everything. But in spite of all this, God was in it for blessing!

I was aware that for many months the Holy Spirit had been interceding for this young man. I had been holding him up before the Father as if he were my own son. Still, I was startled a few weeks before Christmas to hear these English words come forth in prayer: *"The prison bars are broken at Christmas."*

More and more often these same words would come as

I prayed. Of course, Jack was the only person we knew who was in prison at that time, but in our natural thinking we couldn't imagine Jack being given a release. The parole board had been so firm in refusing to reconsider his term.

The night before Christmas Eve we went to the home of Joyce's parents where she and Greg were spending the holidays. Fern had brought a gift of a pretty nightie and slippers to encourage her hopes of a second honeymoon.

We were startled by a knock at the door. Her father opened the door to find Jack, grinning from ear to ear! We felt like Rhoda when Peter was released from the Roman prison by the angel (Acts 12:8). We couldn't believe our eyes!

In a totally unexpected turn of events, Jack was out on a work-release program and he never entered prison doors again! *The prison bars were broken at Christmas!*

God had spoken in prayer through the word of wisdom!

I am happy to tell you that Jack and Joyce now have a beautiful home, a car and a boat. Jack is a respected member of his community today and is always going about doing good. Fern receives a beautiful floral gift every Mother's Day no matter where we are. And for several years, every time we had a big snowfall, I would awaken to find my driveway completely cleared by this outstanding young man.

It is a joy to be with this family. Jack is one of our treasures.

*Bear ye one another's burdens, and so fulfill the law of Christ.* (Galatians 6:2) (KJV)

# 11
# The Scandinavian Story Begins

In the early spring of 1972, I found myself praying much in the Holy Spirit for Norway and Sweden. I assumed I was praying for their governments since I often pray in the Spirit for international events, leaders of countries and affairs of state.

I am a Norwegian by heritage and my wife Fern is Swedish. Both of us grew up hearing relatives talk of events in "the old country," but neither of us dreamed we would one day be ministering there.

Some friends called to say they were going to Europe and Scandinavia on a Full Gospel Business Men's airlift. When they suggested that we join them, we said we would surely pray about it. I remembered that I had prayed in the Spirit concerning Scandinavia, and we were open to whatever the Lord wanted us to do.

Not long after this, a friend came to me after church one Sunday and prophesied, "You will be overseas in a large church where an older man will stand up in the back of the congregation. He will ask you to pray for a son who hasn't been heard from in many years." I took this as a confirmation that we were to proceed in planning for Scandinavia.

We applied for our passports and put in a call to FGBMFI Coordinator Henry Carlson in Chicago. It was the deadline day for reservations, but we got confirmation that we would be on the next flight approximately two weeks later.

We needed luggage and bustled about preparing our wardrobe for late April in northern Europe. Two days before we were to leave, our friends called us again.

"Forget about Scandinavia," they said. "We have decided to go to Mexico City on business and would love to have you join us. Why don't you meet us in Dallas, and we'll fly together to Mexico City for about ten days?"

"Oh!" I replied, "We have all our clothes ready for northern Europe!"

"Not to worry," they said. "You can buy warm-weather clothes in Mexico."

"Well, we'll pray about it," we said. "We'll call you right back tomorrow morning since you'll have to know right away to make your plans."

As we hung up the phone and looked at each other, we immediately knew that we would not be going to Mexico. We both felt the direction of the Holy Spirit, confirming that He wanted us to go to Scandinavia! It would have been fun to be with our friends in a part of the world we had never visited, but we felt a deep commitment to follow the promptings and confirmation of the Holy Spirit.

Our call to our friends was met with regret on their part, but with steadfast assurance on ours. We did not know what was ahead, nor did we care. It was exciting to anticipate an adventure and depend totally on God.

Two days later in Copenhagen, Henry Carlson came to me to designate areas of ministry. He asked me where I would like to go. My reply was, "Norway," because I had always wanted to see the land of my forebears. But Henry suggested that he felt a strong **impression** to send us to central southern Sweden.

That was all I needed to hear!

Henry did not know that for several weeks the Holy Spirit had been whispering to me in that inner voice, "You will be *sent*...You will be *sent*...You will be *sent*...." I recognized the leadership of the Holy Spirit, and Henry's words were another witness to my spirit. I told him I would go wherever I was needed.

On the short plane hop from Copenhagen to Stockholm, Fern and I sat next to a military man. When he mentioned the name of his country, Fern said, "Oh! You are from behind the Iron Curtain."

"Yes," he replied, looking downcast. "We do not have the freedom you Americans enjoy."

"You think Americans are free?" we asked. "They are bound by the same chains of sin and guilt that bind all people, and cannot experience real freedom until they meet Jesus Christ. Only Jesus can set us free from the penalty of sin, and only then can we, as you, know true freedom."

We continued a meaningful discussion until we landed at the Stockholm airport. He received our words graciously and thanked us for sharing this with him. When we parted he gave us a memento of his country which we cherish.

By the time we received our luggage and found the train station in Stockholm, we had to run to catch the train. But when we arrived at our assigned church, the minister was puzzled. It seemed that we were scheduled for another day on his calendar.

As we stood outside on the huge stone steps wondering what to do, a Saab pulled up to an abrupt stop (the only way they stop in Sweden). The driver informed us in quite good English that she had been sent to bring us to another church some miles away.

It was after dark when we arrived, and their meeting was in progress. We could make out the tall white steeple and the beautiful stained glass windows. Inside, we found the church packed with an eager group of about 500. Never will I forget that first evening.

The people seemed to surge with anticipation. I had an interpreter because I do not speak Swedish. This man spoke excellent English (as do all the young people), and I learned that he taught at the local high school. He and his wife were on furlough from mission work in Africa.

Before we departed to a nearby home for a midnight lunch, my interpreter embraced me. I was also informed that when I had lapsed into that heavenly language (tongues), I had been speaking *Swedish!*

The same man was my interpreter during our entire stay in Sweden. In fact, he was never far from me wherever I went. Just before we left Sweden, I found out that I had prayed with him in his native Swedish tongue also. He told me that I had prayed for certain situations that concerned him and told him things that he alone knew!

From that very first night, we had throngs of people coming to our various locations throughout central southern Sweden.

For eight days our schedule consisted of at least two meetings a day, often three, occasionally four. We were giving our testimonies in radio stations and large alcoholic centers, and also conducting question-and-answer sessions in high school classrooms.

I want to tell you about the remarkable experience I had at the largest prison in Sweden, at Kumla.

> *In all thy ways acknowledge him, and he shall direct thy paths.* (Proverbs 3:6, KJV)

# 12
# Kumla

It was our great privilege to stay in the home of Rev. and Mrs. Stig Johansson, who pastored five Baptist churches (which were very close to Pentecostal). Neither he nor his wife Berit knew English. Berit had studied English in high school many years before, but had no opportunity to practice speaking it. This led to many comical situations in communication. Fern finally gave up on learning ingredients and measurements for delicious recipes, though she tasted to determine flour and sugar, etc. Gestures were our basic language combined with expressions you wouldn't believe. Love conquered all barriers here!

For instance, one day Rev. Johansson was trying to communicate to us that we would be ministering at a prison. With fingers crossed over his face, a downcast expression, and hands pulling at imaginary bars, his gestures marked a high point of comedy. Much to our relief he finally made a pencil drawing, and at last we guessed correctly—a prison!

A little later, our interpreter explained that the top security prison at Kumla was entirely underground, and was the state's largest facility for hardened criminals. Rev. Johansson had been unable to arrange any meetings there for a period of years, and was delighted when the officials consented to admit "the Americans."

When we arrived at Kumla Prison, the officials spoke to us in English and explained the security bell system to us. (When the final bell of the day sounded, the doors locked automatically. Anyone still inside would have to remain in the prison for the night.) Then we were led underground to a room where approximately twenty psychiatric prisoners were assembled. Fern played the piano (as she did everywhere we went), and we sang just a bit.

As I spoke through the interpreter, I told of an experience we had with a prisoner in the United States; of his dramatic deliverance from sin and his total commitment to follow Jesus. Three doctors of psychiatry stood by the doorway observing.

Suddenly as I was speaking, a tall blonde young man rose in the rear of the room and marched right to the front. Standing directly in front of me, he said in good English, "I want Jesus to be my Savior!"

I took him to a room across the hall to pray. As we finished praying, a prison guard appeared.

"Please, come quickly!" he urged.

A middle-aged man in the front row had created quite a disturbance. The demons within him were shrieking in a high-pitched voice, "I ruined your meeting! I ruined your meeting!" He was writhing and hollering, while two guards tried to control him. No one knew what to do.

I stopped and quickly observed the situation, breathing the name of Jesus. Perceiving that he was demon possessed, I put my hands on each side of his head, and the Holy Spirit actively joined in prayer.

In a loud voice I commanded the demons to leave him in Jesus' name. "Don't say that Name!" cried one of the demons *in English.* "Spell it, but don't say it!"

I continued to pray forcefully in the name of Jesus and utterances in tongues, and commanded all demons to depart.

"We know we have to go," they cried, "But we have no place. Where shall we go?"

I consigned them to an uninhabited desert part of the earth. The man slumped down in his chair like a wet rag. This man was not an English-speaking person! Demons can speak any language, and had done so on this occasion.

I knew this man wasn't completely delivered, but the first warning bell had rung. We had only seven minutes to get out before the gates automatically locked for the night.

The three doctors wanted to talk to me. They had heard that Pentecostals had power like this, but they had never seen it before. They said they would like to have me minister throughout the prison to small, well-guarded groups.

Oh! We would have liked to stay, but firm plans had already been made for our remaining days in Sweden, and it was not my place to change them. I had a job in the U.S. to get back to though God was already working in me the desire to let go of my secure job and be where He needed me.

Within my spirit welled up a great longing to be able to come back to Sweden as God would direct.

Though we were unable to stay, Pastor Johansson was invited to return regularly to minister to the prisoners. After years of being denied permission, the doors had been opened for ministry at Kumla!

*Behold! I have given you authority and power...over all the power that the enemy [possesses], and nothing shall in any way harm you.* (Luke 10:19)

# 13
# A Prophecy Fulfilled

We were welcomed into a traditional Lutheran church. Its beautiful horseshoe-shaped balcony, immaculately clean, was filled with expectant Swedes. After some songs and preliminaries, I delivered the message the Lord had placed on my heart earlier in the day.

I was almost finished when I was interrupted by a voice in the back of the church. An older man was standing up. With a sobbing voice, he asked me if I would please pray for his son. He hadn't been heard from in many years and his whereabouts were unknown. Before this man departed to be with the Lord, he wanted to see his son once more. All of us were moved by his anguish.

Immediately I remembered the prophecy a friend had spoken to me when we were inquiring of the Lord regarding this trip. I was thrilled to pray for his son, and the Holy Spirit took hold in power! As I marveled at the working of the Holy Spirit, I recognized another mark of confirmation upon my ministry.

In three days a report came back to us that this man's son had returned home unexpectedly. His father was overjoyed!

*And they went forth and preached everywhere, the Lord working with them, and confirming the word with signs following.* (Mark 16:20, KJV)

# 14
# The State Church

Old and magnificent buildings mark the Swedish state churches. Cathedral ceilings, ornate marble altars and splendid, rare chandeliers grace buildings that are attended by only eight or ten old folk once a week. The majority of young Swedes do not exhibit any interest in "religion."

We had been told of this lethargy throughout Scandinavia so from the first meeting our hearts were stirred to find crowds of young people. About fifty percent of our attendance was young people, and they followed us everywhere. If there weren't enough seats, they sat on the floor, in the aisles or directly in front of the altar historically an open area.

In one particular state church, we enjoyed a "grand tour" before our meeting began. The pastor showed us portraits of all the former pastors, hung impressively in the Great Hall. There were many enormous chandeliers unlike any we had ever seen, indescribably beautiful. On either side of a long path from the church's front doors were monuments of the departed faithful. The grandeur of this particular church remains a marvelous memory.

When the meeting began, young people had filled the aisles and the front right up to the altar rail. We noted many of the same faces in all the meetings. This was to be our last meeting in Sweden, and young folk were there by the score.

When I finished speaking, there came occasional utterances in tongues. I wondered just how to proceed, so I paused to pray inviting the audience to join me. The Holy Spirit bore witness to Jesus as Savior, and as I finished my prayer I heard quite a moving about. Opening my eyes, I saw young people surging to the altar, weeping. So many came that they climbed over the altar rail into the "inner sanctum" reserved behind the altar. I did not know what I had said in tongues, but all heaven broke loose!

Not only did salvation appear to them, but many were filled with the Holy Spirit and began to speak with other tongues. It was a very loud and noisy time in such a formal church of "the establishment."

I went from youth to youth, being led by His Spirit in a mighty demonstration of His power. When I had finished praying with a certain young man, my interpreter informed me that he was a student who had been considered "a toughie" and "incorrigible." Now he was weeping in repentance before the Lord! I was later informed of changes that continued in his life confirming this move of the Spirit of God.

God broke through!

He does what no man can do!

*...as servants (slaves) of Christ, doing the will of God heartily and with your whole soul; rendering service readily with goodwill, as to the Lord and not to men.*
(Ephesians 6:6-7)

# 15
# A Park in Oslo

The group from our airlift had disbanded to various European countries, and we had only one day left before we were to meet in Stockholm.

I had been praying much about Oslo for several days, so we concluded that the Lord must have a purpose for us there. We decided to take the train to Oslo for just the day and then go back to Stockholm.

The train journey was very interesting. The passengers kept to themselves, but this was explained to us as a respect for privacy, not snobbishness. Indeed, we found everyone to be very hospitable, opening up if we spoke to them, and a lady across the aisle offered to share some fresh fruit when she discovered we were Americans.

As we disembarked from the train, we inquired about a place to buy the famous Norwegian wool sweaters. It was only a few blocks from the train depot, so we strolled along and finally made our purchase. We weren't in the mood for a meal having eaten excellent food on the train, but decided to have a sandwich in the park near our shopping. We were addressing some picture postcards and wondering where we could find a post box.

I noticed a tall blonde young man cutting across the park in our direction, books under his arm and decided to ask him.

"Pardon me," I inquired very loudly and clearly (hoping this would help him understand), "Can you tell us where we can mail these postcards?"

To our surprise, the only sound that came in reply was a long, high-pitched "OOOOOooooo." This sound continued until finally I said, "In the name of Jesus, SPEAK!"

Immediately the young man said in perfect English, "There is a post box around the next corner over there."

"Do you live there?" we asked.

Once again, the only reply was a high-pitched "OOOOOooooo" until once again we commanded him in Jesus' name to speak.

Every remark we made elicited this same high-pitched sound until the name that is higher than any other name was spoken. It was apparent that a demon spirit was the cause of this speech impediment. (I finally instructed him to say the name of Jesus himself; and every time he said "Jesus," he was indeed able to speak.)

At the name of Jesus, he informed us that he was a student on his way to a class at the University near the park. He was studying *"Comparative Religions."*

We knew then that we were in the right place at the right time.

At the name of Jesus, he told us that he wanted to study religions to find out "who was the true God!"

It was a joy to fulfill our "divine appointment" by telling him of the one who is the truth! We told him of Jesus and His claims on his life.

He was nearly late for his class by this time, and anxious to be on his way. Not wishing to detain him, we left him with these words, "When you confess Jesus as your Lord and Savior, you will be free from your speech impediment."

As we hurried to catch the night train to Stockholm, we rejoiced in a "mission accomplished!"

# 16
# The Comforter

Weariness overtook us as we boarded the train to Stockholm. Eight days of nonstop ministry had afforded us little time to rest. We couldn't sit together as the train was very crowded. Parents were holding their children on their laps and we were thankful to even get a seat.

We wished we had had the foresight to reserve a berth overnight so we could catch up on sleep. But our trip to Oslo had been hastily arranged.

I tugged at the sleeve of the trainman as he came to validate tickets.

"We would like to have sleeping accommodations. Is this possible, sir?"

"All full. Sorry," was his reply.

Five or ten minutes went by and the train finally got underway. The sun had set when I noticed the trainman beckoning me. I rose and met him in a corridor. He informed me that a woman was getting off at the next stop and we could have her berth. He said there would be no charge, as she had paid her way to Stockholm and suddenly decided to change her plans!

We knew there were many people on that overnight trip who would have liked some rest, and perhaps some who needed it more than we. Yet our Father had us in mind and specifically saw to our comfort.

As the train sped toward Stockholm, the Comforter (Blanket) surrounded us and we felt absolutely abandoned to His love and care.

*Take care of others and God will take care of you.*

# 17
# A Stronger Commitment

Our time in Scandinavia was drawing to a close, but Pastor Stig Johansson and his wife Berit begged us to stay. "Why leave now?" they asked. "We have never before seen the Lord move in such a fashion."

I explained that I had to get back to my job and that our tickets were good only for certain dates. At the train station in Hallsberg, we bade one another goodbye with tears in our eyes. We would look forward to seeing one another again in God's timing.

Fern and I returned home with a stronger commitment to serve God with all our strength, and to be utterly dependent on the Holy Spirit.

> ...the (Holy) Spirit comes to our aid and bears us up in our weakness; for we do not know what prayer to offer nor how to offer it worthily as we ought, but the Spirit Himself goes to meet our supplication and pleads in our behalf with unspeakable yearnings and groanings too deep for utterance. And he who searches the hearts of men knows what is in the mind of the (Holy) Spirit --what His intent is-- because the Spirit intercedes and pleads [before God] in behalf of the saints according to and in harmony with God's will. (Romans 8:26-27)